I was born on

at

The time was

I was delivered by

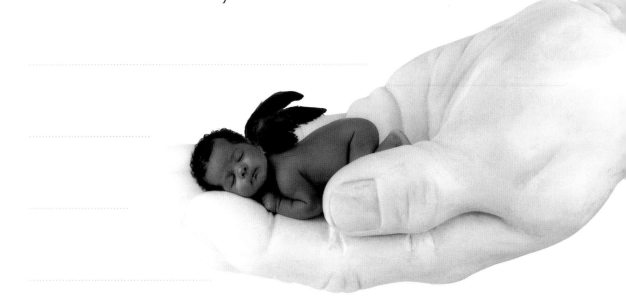

I weighed   and measured

My eyes were

My hair was

Mementos

My Birth Announcement

A lock of hair

My hospital tag

Newspaper Clippings

What was happening in the world

Photographs

Comments

Mother ....

....

....

....

....

Father ....

....

....

....

Special Messages

Family ....

....

....

....

Friends ....

....

....

....

Visitors and Gifts

Signs

Star Sign ....

Chinese Year ....

Birth Stone ....

Birth Flower ....

Comments ....

....

....

....

Naming

My full name is ....

My name was chosen by ....

because ....

My pet names are ....

Ceremonies celebrating my birth ....

....

Comments ....

....

....

....

Photographs

My Family Tree

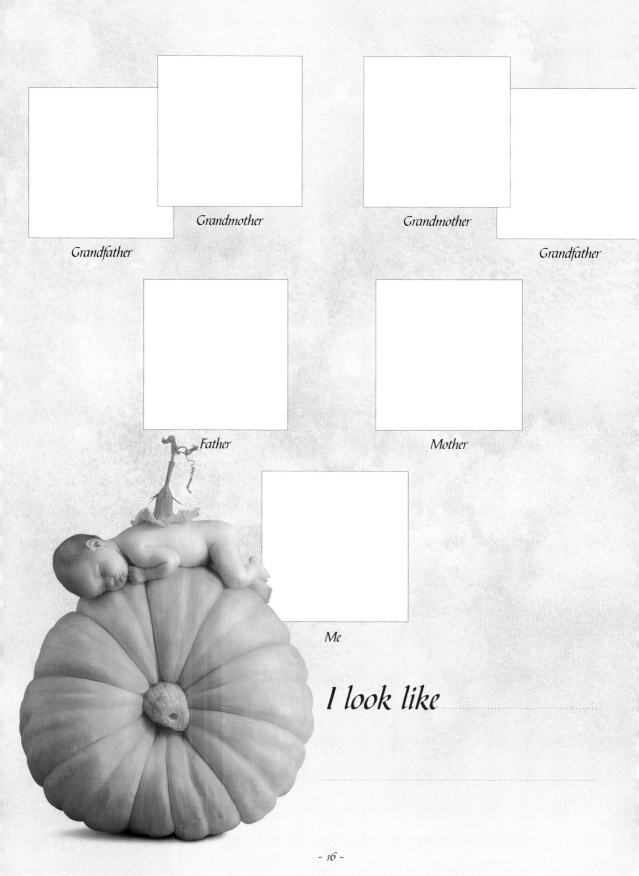

Grandfather

Grandmother

Grandmother

Grandfather

Father

Mother

Me

I look like ....

....

Photographs

Brothers and Sisters

Three Months

Weight ....

Length ....

Comments ....

....

....

....

....

....

....

Photographs

Six Months

Weight .... *Length* ....

Comments ....

....

....

....

....

....

Photographs

Nine Months

Weight ....

Length ....

Comments ....

....

....

....

....

....

....

Photographs

Milestones

I first smiled ....

laughed ....

grasped a toy ....

I slept through the night ....

I held my head up ....

rolled over ....

sat up ....

Comments ....

....

....

....

I first crawled ....

stood up ....

walked ....

My first tooth ....

My first word ....

Comments ....

Food

My first solid food ....

....

I was weaned ....

I drank from a cup ....

Finger food ....

I fed myself ....

I like

I don't like

My First Christmas

was at ....

Other people there ....

....

....

My presents ....

....

Photographs

My First Vacation

was at ....

Date ....

The weather was ....

Other people there ....

....

....

....

Comments ....

....

....

....

Photographs

My First Birthday

I live at ....

My height is .... Weight ....

Sayings ....

Toys ....

....

Pets ....

Books ....

....

My Party

Date ....

Where held ....

Friends and relations there ....

....

....

My presents ....

....

....

....

Photographs

Clothes

The first time I dressed myself ....

I wore ....

....

My favorite dress-ups ....

....

I won't wear ....

....

Comments ....

....

....

....

Photographs

Favorites

Music

....

....

Rhymes

....

....

Clothes

....

....

Animals

....

....

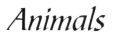

Activities

Television programs

I really don't like

Best Friends

Comments

....

....

....

Photo

One Year

....

....

....

Photo

Two Years

Photo

Three Years

....

....

Photo

Photo

Four Years

Five Years

My Second Birthday

I live at ....

My height is .... Weight ....

Sayings ....

Toys ....

....

Pets ....

....

Books ....

My Party

Date ....

Where held ....

Friends and relations there ....

....

....

My presents ....

....

....

....

Photographs

My Third Birthday

I live at ....

My height is .... Weight ....

Sayings ....

....

....

Toys ....

....

Pets ....

....

 Books ....

....

My Party

Date ....

Where held ....

Friends and relations there ....

....

....

....

My presents ....

....

....

Photographs

My Fourth Birthday

I live at ....

My height is .... Weight ....

Sayings ....

....

Toys ....

....

Pets ....

....

Books ....

....

....

My Party

Date ....

Where held ....

Friends and relations there ....

....

....

....

My presents ....

....

....

....

Photographs

Pre-School

My first day at pre-school was on ....

....

at ....

My friends are ....

....

....

Comments ....

....

....

Photographs

My Fifth Birthday

I live at ....

My height is .... Weight ....

Sayings ....

....

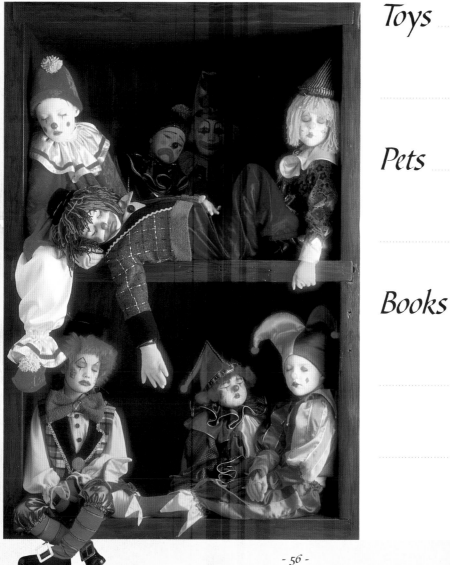

Toys ....

....

Pets ....

....

Books ....

....

....

My Party

Date ....

Where held ....

Friends and relations there

....

....

....

....

My presents ....

....

....

....

Photographs

Kindergarten

I started on ....

at ....

My teacher is ....

Comments ....

A ....

....

....

B

....

C D E F

Photographs

Drawings

K L M N

Writing

I could recite the alphabet ....

....

I started to write ....

I began to read ....

My writing ....

....

....

....

....

S T U V

Health

Immunization

Age	Vaccine	Date given

Allergies

Illnesses

Comments

My Height

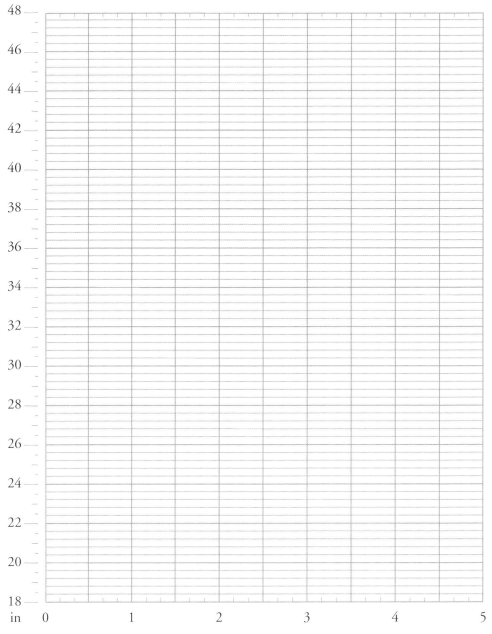

Age (Years)

My Weight

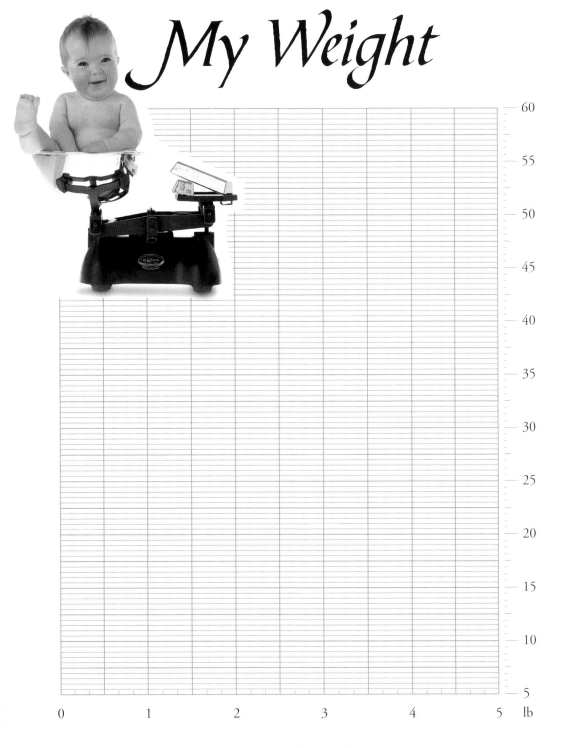

60
55
50
45
40
35
30
25
20
15
10
5

0   1   2   3   4   5 lb

Age (Years)

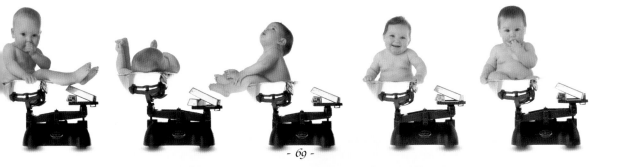

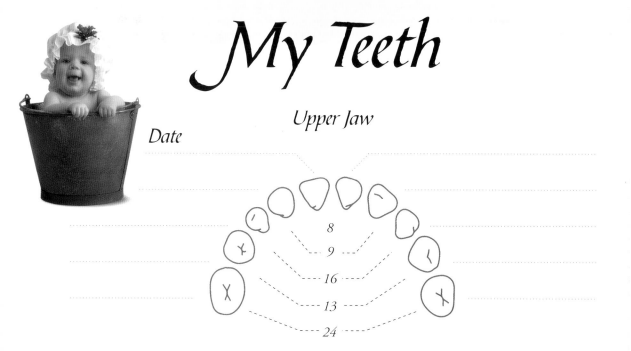

My Teeth

Upper Jaw

Date

8
9
16
13
24

Months

24
13
16
10
7

Date

Lower Jaw

Visits to the dentist

The Tooth Fairy's Page

I lost my first tooth ....

My second tooth ....

The Tooth Fairy left me ....

....

Comments ....

....

....

....

My Handprints

At birth

At five years

My Footprints

At birth

At five years

Birth Stones

January	Garnet – constancy, truth
February	Amethyst – sincerity, humility
March	Aquamarine – courage, energy
April	Diamond – innocence, success
May	Emerald – tranquillity
June	Pearl – preciousness, purity
July	Ruby – freedom from care, chastity
August	Moonstone – joy
September	Sapphire – hope, chastity
October	Opal – reflecting every mood
November	Topaz – fidelity, loyalty
December	Turquoise – love, success

Flowers

January	Snowdrop – pure and gentle
February	Carnation – bold and brave
March	Violet – modest
April	Lily – virtuous
May	Hawthorn – bright and hopeful
June	Rose – beautiful
July	Daisy – wide-eyed and innocent
August	Poppy – peaceful
September	Morning Glory – easily contented
October	Cosmos – ambitious
November	Chrysanthemum – sassy and cheerful
December	Holly – full of foresight

Star Signs

Capricorn
22 December–20 January
Resourceful, self-sufficient, responsible

Aquarius
21 January–18 February
Cares greatly for others, very emotional under cool exterior

Pisces
19 February–19 March
Imaginative, sympathetic, tolerant

Aries
20 March–20 April
Brave, courageous, energetic, loyal

Taurus
21 April–21 May
Sensible, loves peace and stability

Gemini
22 May–21 June
Unpredictable, lively, charming, witty

Cancer
22 June–22 July
Loves security and comfort

Leo
23 July–23 August
Idealistic, romantic, honorable, loyal

Virgo
24 August–23 September
Shy, sensitive, values knowledge

Libra
24 September–23 October
Diplomatic, full of charm and style

Scorpio
24 October–22 November
Compassionate, proud, determined

Sagittarius
23 November–21 December
Bold, impulsive, seeks adventure

Comments

Photographs

Comments

Photographs

ANNE GEDDES ®

www.annegeddes.com

© 2001 Anne Geddes

The right of Anne Geddes to be identified as the Author
of the Work has been asserted by her in accordance
with the Copyright, Designs and Patents Act 1988.

First published in 2001 by Photogenique Publishers
(a division of Hodder Moa Beckett)
Studio 3.11, Axis Building, 1 Cleveland Road
Parnell, Auckland, New Zealand

This edition published in North America in 2001
by Andrews McMeel Publishing
4520 Main Street, Kansas City, MO 64111-7701
2nd Printing, 2002
Produced by Kel Geddes
Color separations by Image Centre
Printed in China by Midas Printing Ltd, Hong Kong

ISBN 0-7407-1806-1